HAPPY THANKSGIVING

THIS BOOK BELONGS TO

TEST YOUR COLOR SUPPLIES ON THIS PAGE TO SEE HOW THEY REACT TO THE PAPER

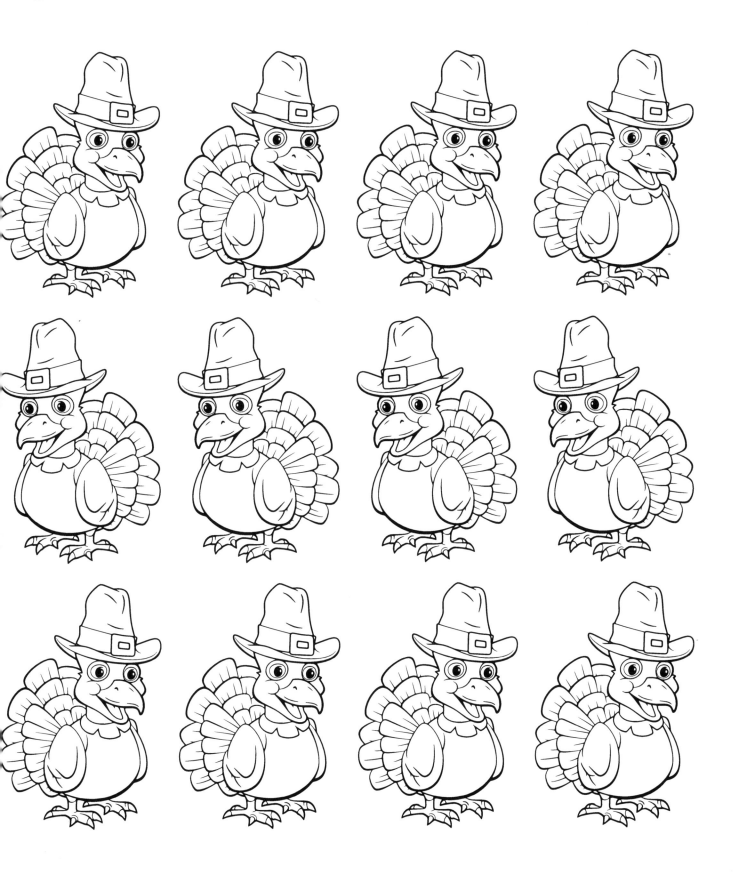

THANKSGIVING

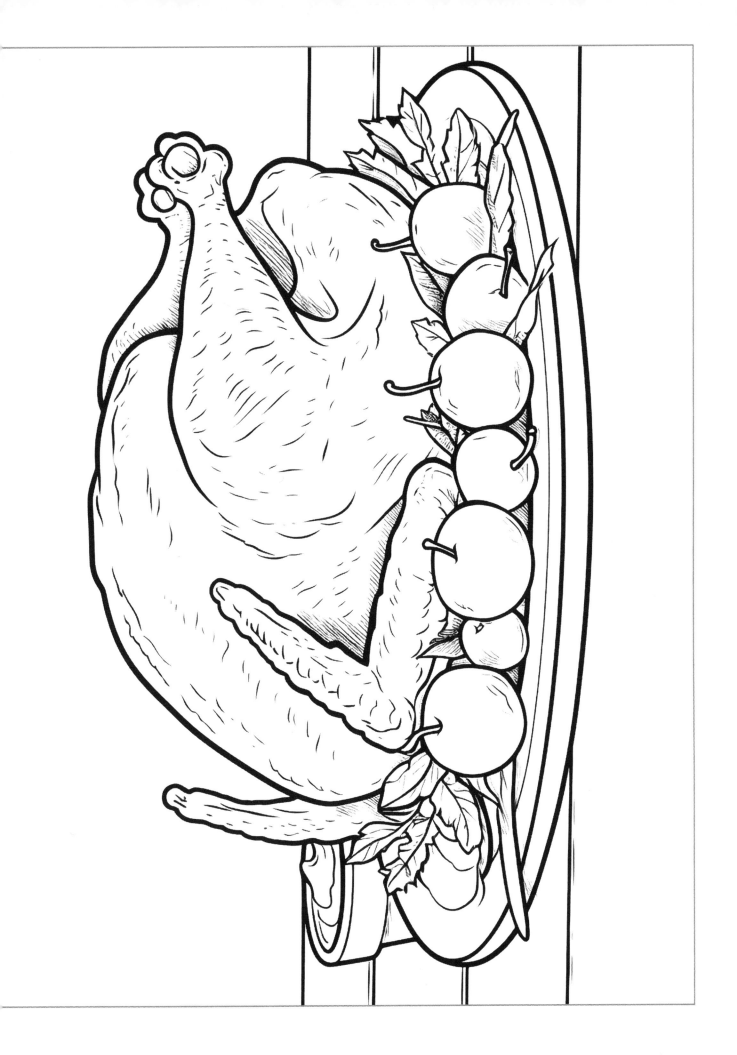

TURKEY DAY!

HAPPY TURKEY DAY!!

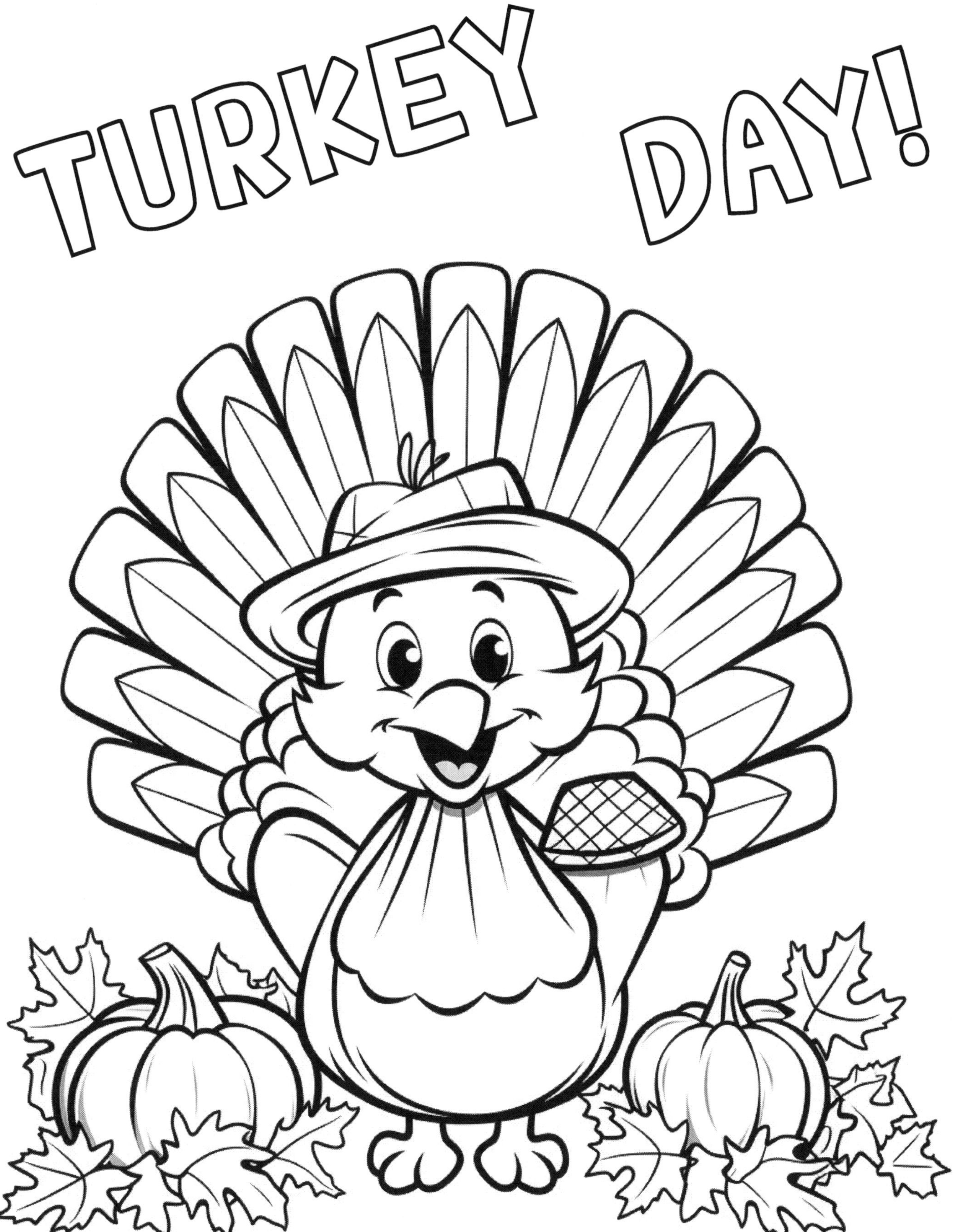
TURKEY DAY!

HAPPY THANKSGIVING

HAPPY TURKEY

HAPPY TURKEY

HAPPY THANKSGIVING

Happy

Thanksgiving!

TURKEY

HAPPY TURKEY

THANKSGIVING

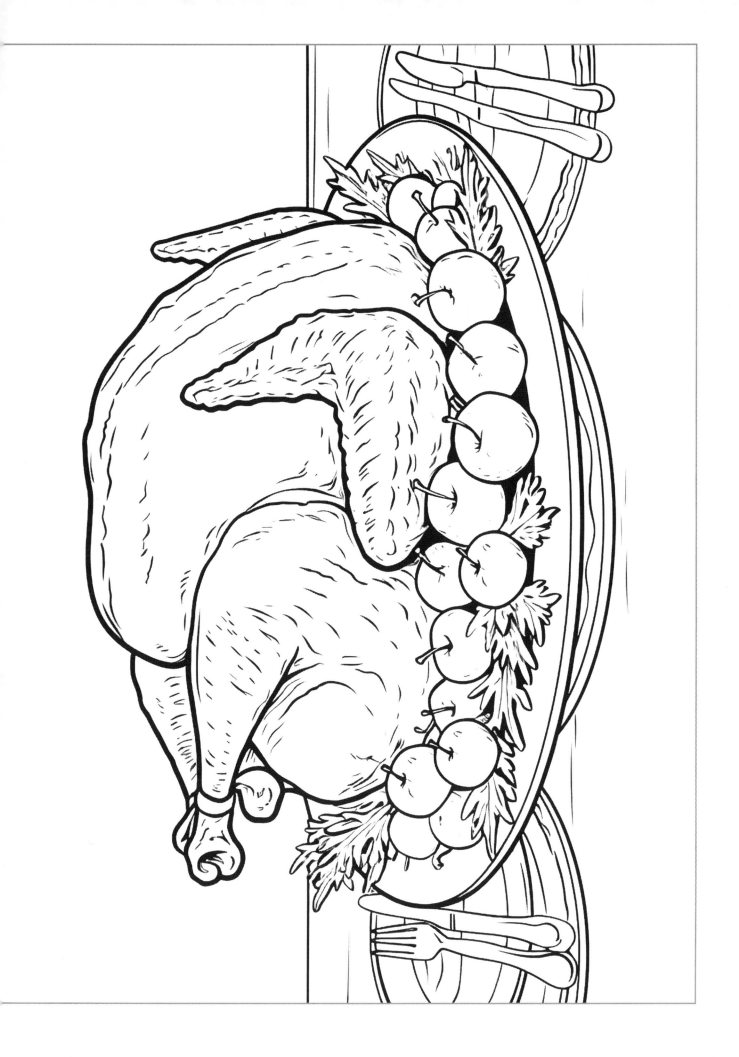

HAPPY TURKEY

HAPPY TURKEY

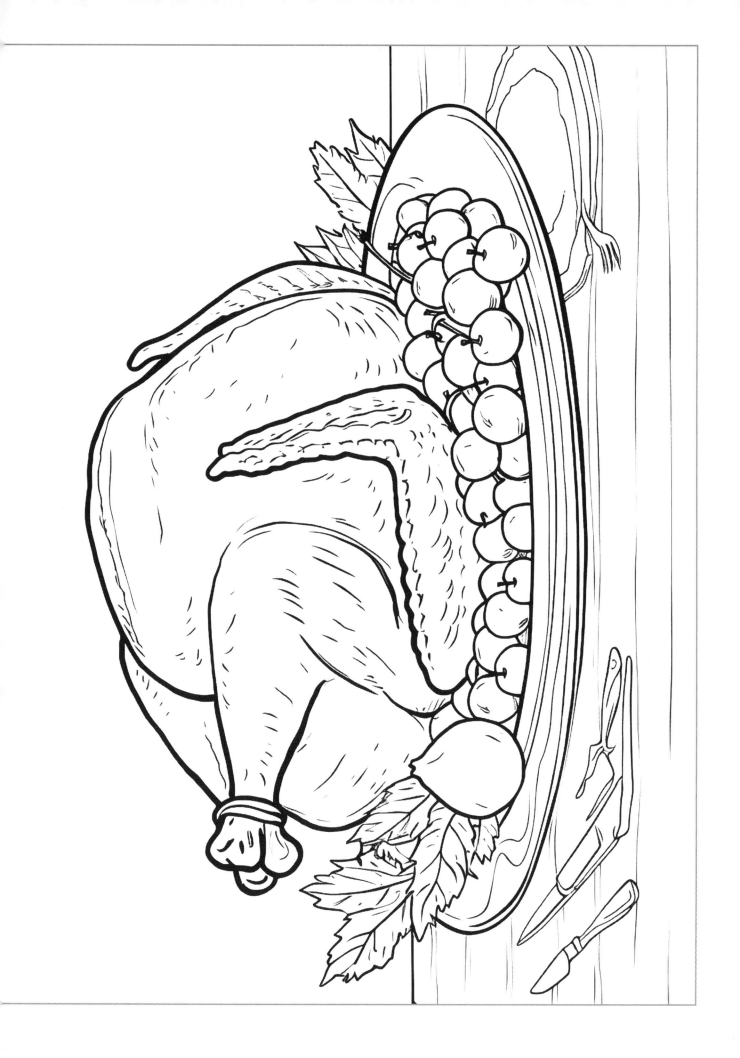

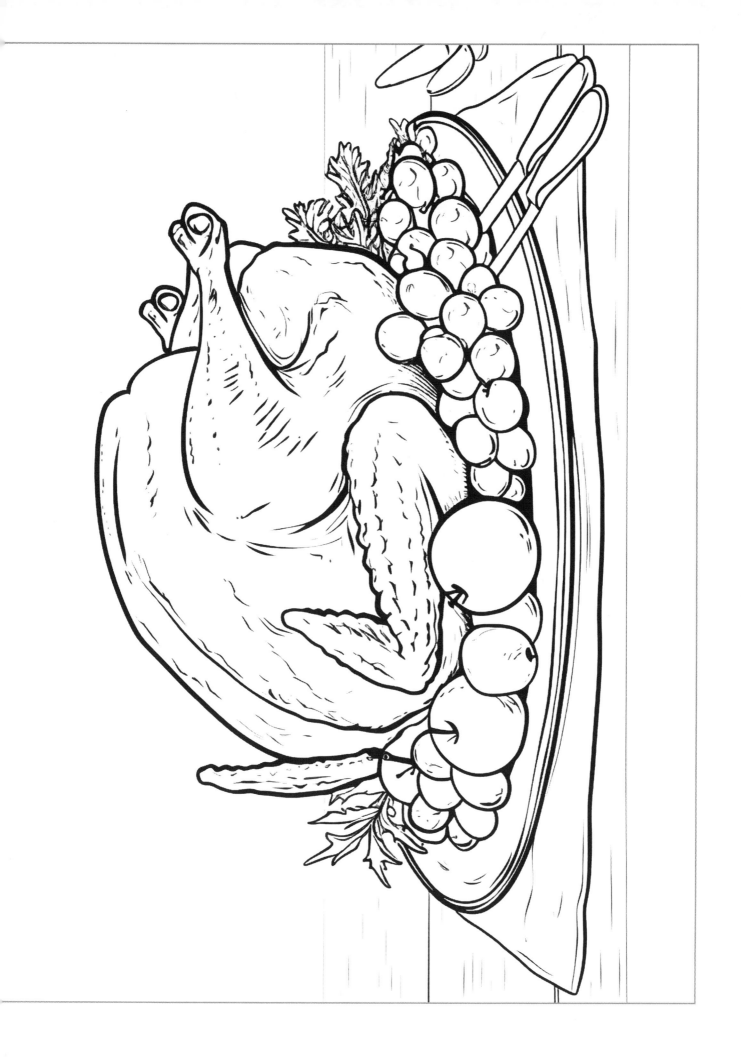

Made in United States
Troutdale, OR
10/18/2024

23914361R00064